Cambridgeshire Libraries

WITHDRAWN FROM STOCK

Cambridge Libraries, Archives and Information Service

This book is due for return on or before the latest date shown above, but may be renewed up to three times unless it has been requested by another customer.

Books can be renewed -
in person at your local library

 Cambridgeshire County Council

Online www.cambridgeshire.gov.uk/library

Please note that charges are made on overdue books.

Cambridgeshire Libraries

WITHDRAWN FROM STOCK

P0010 01008 8455

The Genius Of THE VIKINGS

CLEVER IDEAS AND INVENTIONS FROM PAST CIVILISATIONS

SONYA NEWLAND

W
FRANKLIN WATTS
LONDON · SYDNEY

Franklin Watts

First published in Great Britain in 2019 by
The Watts Publishing Group

Copyright © The Watts Publishing Group, 2019

 Produced for Watts by
White-Thomson Publishing Ltd
www.wtpub.co.uk

All rights reserved.

Editor: Sonya Newland
Consultant: Philip Parker
Series Designer: Rocket Design (East Anglia) Ltd
Designer: Clare Nicholas

ISBN: 978 1 4451 6116 7 (HB) 978 1 4451 6114 3 (PB)
10 9 8 7 6 5 4 3 2 1

Franklin Watts
An imprint of
Hachette Children's Group
Part of The Watts Publishing Group
Carmelite House
50 Victoria Embankment
London EC4Y 0DZ

An Hachette UK Company
www.hachette.co.uk

www.franklinwatts.co.uk

Printed in China

Picture acknowledgements:
Alamy: Heritage Image Partnership Ltd cover, 21, Chronicle 5, National Geographic Creative 15, Dorling Kindersley Ltd 22, North Wind Picture Archives 24, Art Collection 3 25, Prisma Archivo 26; Julian Baker: 6–7, 10, 12; Getty Images: Andy Crawford 4, Heritage Images 13b, Werner Forman 14r, 28; iStock: gremlin 11b, Himagine 13t, Elenarts 18, Tony Baggett 27; Shutterstock: goga18128 7, Algol 8, lovelypeace 9, Aleksandr Pobedimskiy 11t, Tony Baggett 14l, yanami 16–17, GTS Productions 19, elxeneize 20, Drakuliren 23, Alexander A.Trofimov 29.

All design elements from Shutterstock.

Every effort has been made to clear copyright. Should there be any inadvertent omission, please apply to the publisher for rectification.

The website addresses (URLs) included in this book were valid at the time of going to press.
However, it is possible that contents or addresses may have changed since the publication of this book.
No responsibility for any such changes can be accepted by either the author or the publisher.

CONTENTS

THE VIKINGS — 4
THE VIKING LONGSHIP — 6
SAILS AND KEELS — 8
COMPASSES — 10
EXPLORATION — 12
TRADE — 14
BATTLE-AXES — 16
SHIELDS — 18
LAW AND DEMOCRACY — 20
LANGUAGE — 22
SKIING — 24
PERSONAL GROOMING — 26
VIKING SAGAS — 28
GLOSSARY — 30
TIMELINE — 31
INDEX AND FURTHER INFORMATION — 32

THE VIKINGS

Who?

The people known as Norsemen ('men from the north') came from the part of northern Europe we call Scandinavia, which includes Denmark, Norway and Sweden. In their homeland, the Norsemen were farmers and fishermen. However, they were also skilled sailors, and in the eighth century they began sailing along the coast of Europe, plundering any settlements they came across. This behaviour earned them the nickname *vikingr*, which means 'pirate' in the Old Norse language. Today, we still refer to them as Vikings.

Viking helmets did not have horns, although they are often shown with them in modern pictures.

What happened?

The Vikings began raiding British coastal villages in the late eighth century. At first, they simply took what they wanted and sailed away again. But by the middle of the ninth century, the Vikings wanted to settle in England. In CE 886, King Alfred of Wessex reached an agreement with the Vikings. They would be allowed to live in a certain part of the country. This large area of Viking influence became known as the Danelaw.

Despite this early agreement, over the next 200 years there were many shifts in power as the native Anglo-Saxons and the Vikings fought fiercely over control of Britain. The Viking Age is considered to have ended in 1066, when the French duke William of Normandy invaded and conquered England.

While all this was going on, the Vikings were also raiding, trading and settling in other parts of the world. Their legacy can be seen far and wide.

This picture shows King Alfred's ships fighting the Vikings at sea. The two sides eventually reached an agreement.

THE VIKING LONGSHIP

The Vikings are most famous for their lightweight wooden boats, called longships. These cleverly designed vessels allowed the Vikings to travel further and faster than almost anyone else at the time.

How long were longships?

One of the longest and most powerful longships that we know of was called *Ormen Lange* ('Long Serpent'). It might have been more than 45 m long, with 34 pairs of oars. That's longer than four buses end to end. However, a typical longship was about 20—23 m in length. The Vikings built their ships with shallow hulls, which meant they could travel in shallow water such as rivers. This allowed them to make surprise raids in places no one expected them to reach. Their speedy attacking technique was also helped by the rudder, which was mounted on the side of the longship to allow the boat to be pulled ashore quickly and easily.

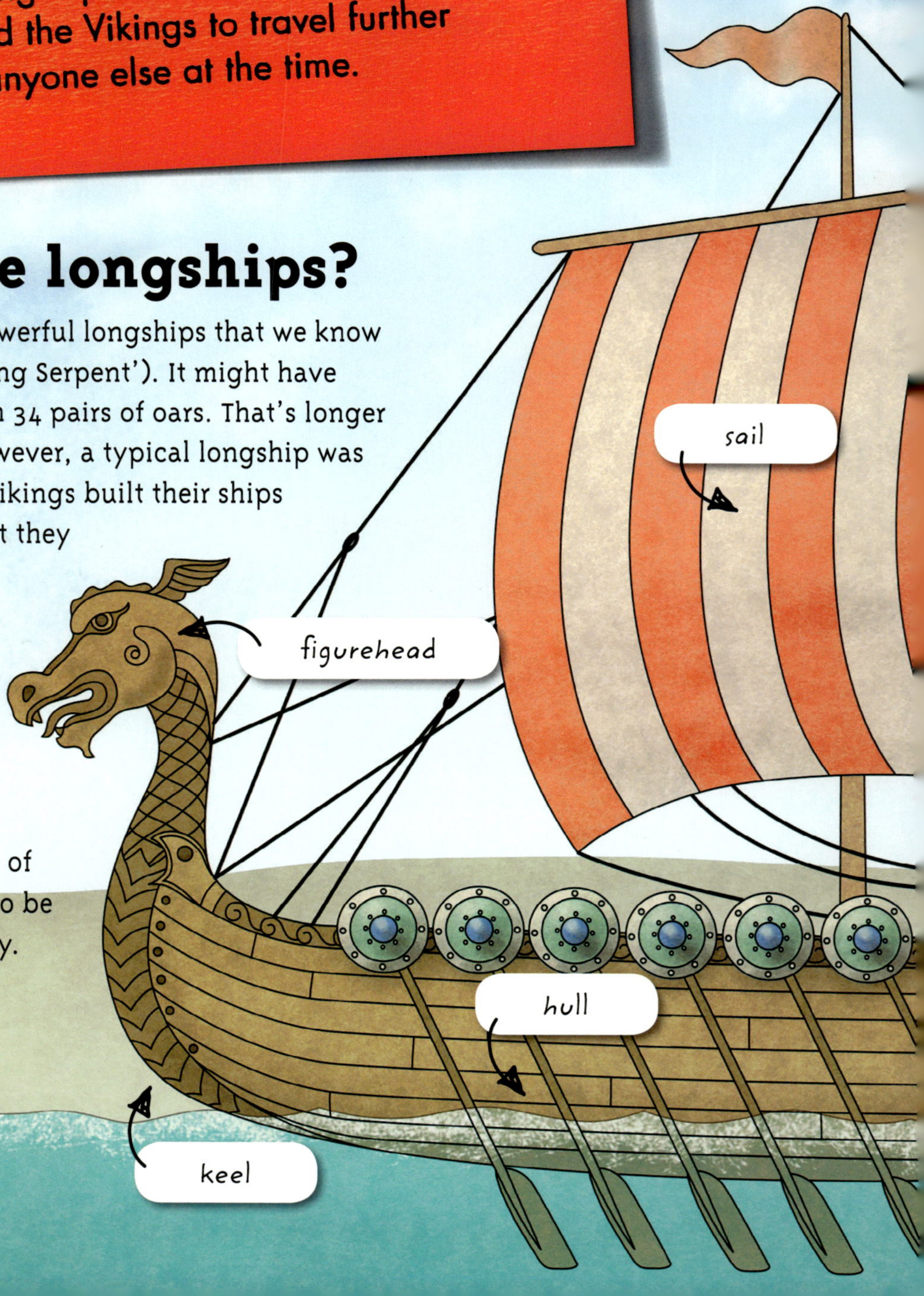

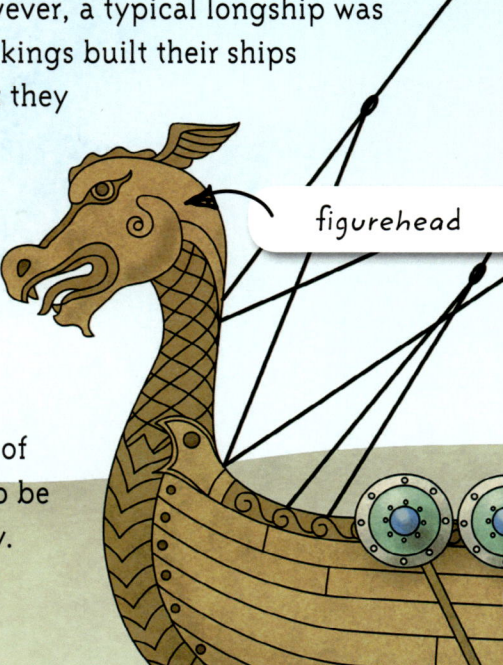

(((BRAIN WAVE)))

Most ships at the time were nailed together, but Viking longships were 'clinker' built. This meant that instead of using nails, the planks were overlapped and joined with iron rivets. This made the ship much more flexible, so it could bend with the pressure of the water.

A Viking crew

Longships had a row of oars on each side, usually powered by between 15 and 60 men. There were no cabins for the crew to take shelter in — they ate and slept on deck. Each crew member took a chest to keep his belongings in. These may have doubled up as seats for the rowers if the boat wasn't fitted with seating planks. Because longships were light, they could travel quickly and be manoeuvred easily by the oarsmen.

The Vikings may have believed that the dragon heads protected the ship and crew from evil spirits.

oars

WOW!

The Vikings carved fierce-looking figureheads at the front and back of their longships. These were often in the shape of dragons, which is why longships are sometimes called dragonboats.

SAILS AND KEELS

At first, the Vikings just explored and raided coastal areas not far from their native Scandinavia. Later, they developed technology that improved their longships so that they could go much faster and travel further afield.

Setting sail

Longships were not only powered by men-at-oars. They also had a huge square sail, made of rough woven wool, attached to a tall mast. The sail could measure up to 11 m across, and it gave the longship much greater speed than manpower alone. It had the added advantage of allowing the Vikings to save their strength for the attack when they arrived!

A kind of wooden pole called a beitass was attached to the sail. This braced it against strong winds and allowed the sail to be moved so the ship could turn as the wind changed, and keep going in the right direction.

At full sail, a Viking ship averaged speeds of 15 km/h.

Inventing the keel

Early Viking boats were not very stable and often capsized in rough water. The Vikings changed that with one simple invention — the keel. This strip of timber fixed along the bottom of the longship made it much more stable, and allowed the Vikings to set out to sea instead of being confined to rivers and coastlines. A whole new world opened up to the Norsemen, with opportunities for exploration, raiding and trade.

Most of what we know about longships comes from archaeological finds in Scandinavia. This is the Oseberg Ship, discovered in a Viking burial mound in Norway.

WOW!

Experienced Viking sailors could tell when land was close by watching how sea birds overhead behaved, or by looking at the colour of the water.

COMPASSES

To be successful explorers, invaders and traders, the Vikings had to have good navigational aids. They invented an amazing device called a sun compass to help them find their way across the sea.

Sailing by the Sun

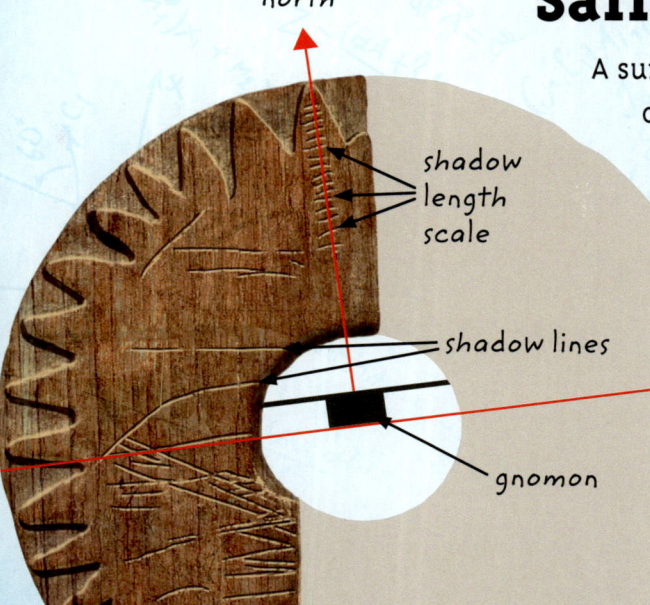

A sun compass was a simple instrument made up of a flat circular wooden disc (the 'shadow board') with a hole in the middle. A peg called a 'gnomon' was inserted into the hole so it stood upright, a bit like a sundial. As the shadow of the gnomon fell across the disc, sailors marked its position. They did this every hour from sunrise to sunset, then they drew a line to connect the points in a curve. This 'gnomon line' allowed the Vikings to work out their latitude while at sea.

Experts have used a part of a sun compass that has been discovered to work out how the Vikings used it to navigate.

WOW!

The Vikings realised that they needed to adapt the sun compass to allow for the Sun being at different heights at different times of year. They carried gnomons of different sizes to help them do this.

Knowledge of the Earth

The mineral magnetite was plentiful in Scandinavia, and the Vikings may have used it to make a type of magnetic compass. They knew that the Sun rose in the east and set in the west. They also knew that in their part of the world, the Sun was in the south at midday. This knowledge may have allowed them to create a magnetic compass to find their way even when there was no sunlight.

The mineral magnetite is also known as lodestone. 'Lode' meant 'journey' and the mineral got this name because of its early use in compasses.

Out at sea, with no landmarks, Viking sailors had to rely on devices such as compasses to identify their position and find their way.

EXPLORATION

The development of the longship and the compass allowed the Vikings to become pioneers in other ways. They were among the first people to travel far afield and discover and colonise other lands. They sailed the seas as far south as North Africa and east to what is now Russia.

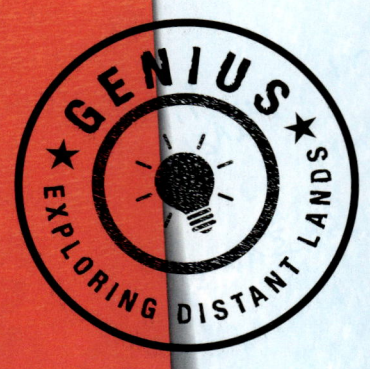

Exploring Iceland

One of the first countries the Vikings discovered was Iceland, which was sighted by a Norseman called Naddod in the 830s or 840s. In around CE 860, the Viking explorer Gardar Svavarsson sailed all the way round it, proving that it was an island. Vikings sagas (see page 28) tell how when Svavarsson left, one of his men, Náttfari, stayed behind and made Iceland his home. By CE 930, around 10,000 Vikings had settled there.

At the height of the Vikings' power, their settlements could be found from North America to Russia.

Greenland

In around CE 980, a Viking called Erik the Red was banished from Iceland after he killed someone. After setting sail in CE 982, he arrived at a place he later called Greenland. He thought this pleasant name would make people want to live there. When his exile ended three years later, Erik returned to Iceland. He encouraged other Vikings to go back to Greenland with him to explore and settle in this area.

A statue of Erik the Red in Greenland

Across the Atlantic

Erik the Red's son, Leif Eriksson, was an even greater explorer. Setting out from Greenland, he sailed to what we now call North America. The Vikings called this country Vinland because of all the grapevines that grew there. The Viking homeland in Scandinavia was 5,000 km away across the Atlantic, making communication with the new outpost an incredible achievement.

WOW!

To make fire wherever they went, the Vikings collected a type of fungus from the bark of trees. They boiled it in urine for a few days, then hammered it into a flammable material a bit like felt, which they lit using flint and steel to create sparks.

Leif Eriksson reached North America in around CE 1000.

TRADE

As the Vikings reached new lands, they came into contact with different peoples and discovered resources that they could not produce for themselves. It wasn't long before the Vikings realised they could make themselves rich by trading with these countries.

The importance of trade

The exchange of goods and ideas became very important in Viking times. Trade helped form relationships with other cultures and improved life back home by increasing personal wealth. The Vikings were the leading traders of the time. They traded with cultures in the Middle East such as the Arabs, as well as with other European civilisations.

After the Vikings settled in England they began issuing coins like the Anglo-Saxons did, although using plain pieces of silver was more common.

(((BRAIN WAVE)))

The Vikings engaged in a type of trade called 'bullion economy', where weighed pieces of silver – and sometimes gold – were used as money. Viking traders had special folding scales to weigh the precious metal.

Viking scales like this could weigh pieces of silver very accurately.

Trade routes and goods

The Vikings also established trade routes (see map on page 12) to and from the area that is now Russia, along the Volga River. The goods that the Vikings traded in these areas included timber, wheat, wool, tin, honey, leather and ivory from walrus tusks. They exchanged these for items such as silver, silk, wine, spices, glass and pottery.

Trading in slaves

The Vikings were also slave traders, and slaves — called 'thralls' — were one of their most valuable commodities. Some slaves came from conquered territories in Eastern Europe and Britain, but others were Vikings themselves: men and women who had been enslaved as a punishment for committing murder or theft.

A Viking selling a slave girl to a Persian merchant. Traded goods, such as silk and furs, can be seen on the ground.

BATTLE-AXES

The Vikings were a warrior people, and having effective weapons was a matter of life and death. Digging iron from the earth was a complicated process, so only the richest Vikings could afford a full set of weapons and armour.

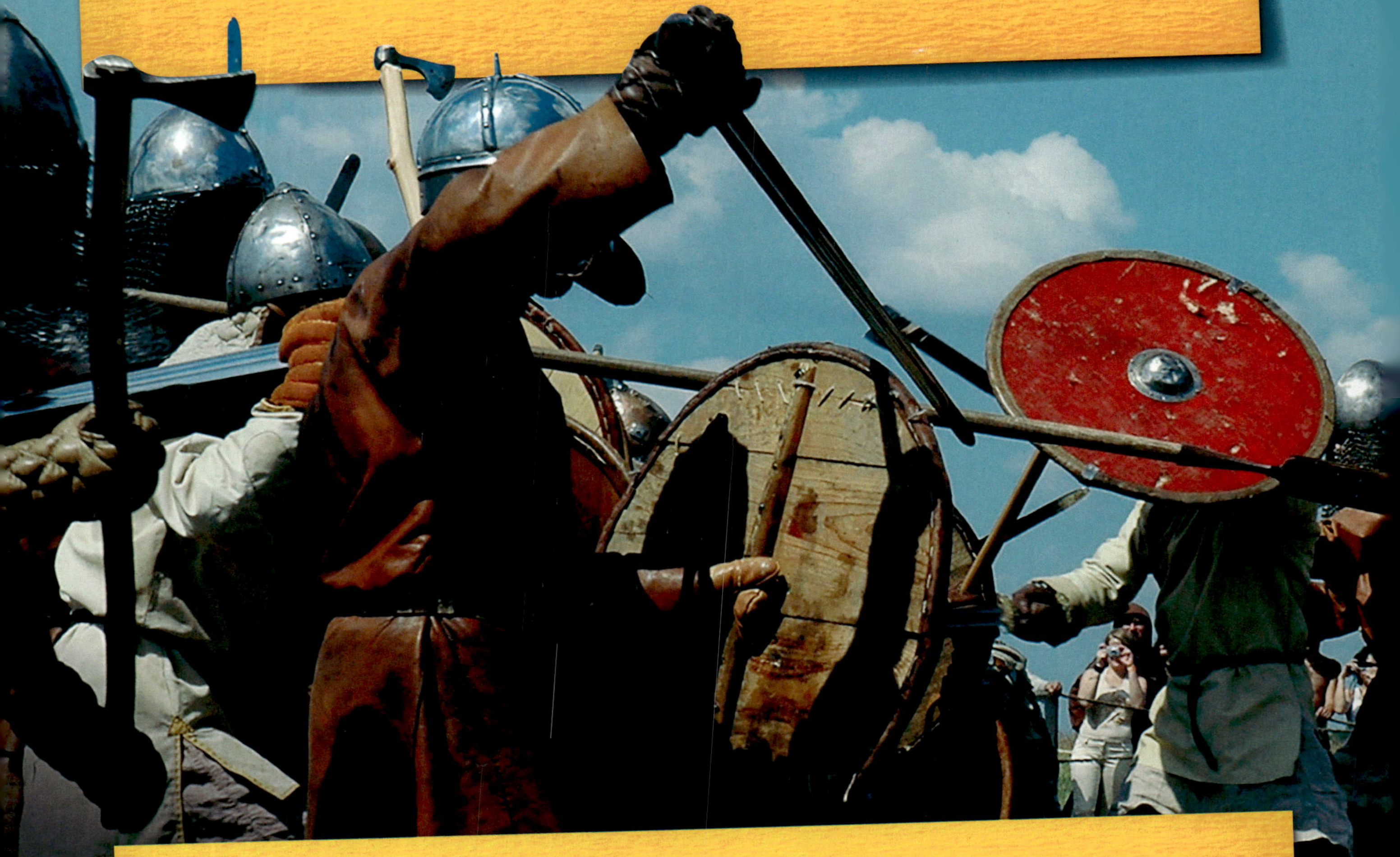

Weapon wardrobe

A wealthy Viking might own a sword, a spear and a bow and arrows, as well as a shield, helmet and chainmail armour. Most Vikings carried much less weaponry than this, but almost all of them owned an axe. They developed axes into useful and terrifying weapons, and used them in imaginative ways!

On the battlefield

Axes started out as simple tools used for chopping wood, but over the years the Vikings adapted them to become unique weapons. Axes were made larger and broader so that they could do more damage. Some battle-axes had a hook, which was used to catch an enemy by his foot or shield before bringing the blade down on him.

(((Brain Wave)))

In late Viking times, a large, two-handed axe was invented. This meant that the soldier could not hold a shield at the same time. To counteract this, the Vikings invented a new battle tactic in which the man holding the axe would stay behind a front line of warriors, then rush out to surprise the enemy.

The axe was the most common weapon used by the Vikings in battle.

SHIELDS

The circular Viking shield was carefully made to provide excellent protection. It was created especially with the Vikings' methods of attack – and defence – in mind.

GENIUS ★ WELL-PROTECTED WARRIORS

Shield construction

Viking shields were about 75–90 cm wide. They were made of seven or eight thin strips of wood. These may have been strengthened with iron bands. Viking shields did not have straps to secure them to the soldier's arm. Instead, there was a hole in the middle where an iron handle was attached. An iron dome called a 'boss' covered the hole at the front.

Hanging shields over the edge of the longship protected the sides from damage by rocks and the lashing waves.

WOW!

The Vikings would often hang their shields over the sides of the longship. This kept them out of the way but still easily accessible if the oarsmen needed them in a hurry.

Battle tactics

On the battlefield, Viking warriors would form lines of defence. They would hold up their shields so that they overlapped. This created a strong wall that the enemy found hard to penetrate. The wood that the shields were made from was thin and flexible, making it less likely to be split by a blow from an enemy weapon.

(((Brain Wave)))

The size of a shield was important: too small and it wouldn't provide enough protection; too large and it would be too heavy and difficult to handle. Vikings probably tailored the size of their shields to match their own strength and size.

This modern reconstruction of a Viking battle shows soldiers with overlapping shields. Viking shields may have been painted with simple patterns.

LAW AND DEMOCRACY

The Vikings helped to establish a system of law and order in the part of England known as the Danelaw (see page 5), which they ruled over for many years. Many words from Old Norse are related to the law, including 'wrong' and 'loan' as well as the word 'law' itself.

Things

In order to make and keep laws, assemblies known as Things were held across Scandinavia and in many other places where the Vikings settled. A Thing was a body of men who had the power to create local laws and put people on trial for crimes. It had some of the powers that a modern parliament has, as well as those of a court of law. All non-enslaved Norsemen could attend their local Thing.

TEST of TIME

In CE 930, the Vikings established the Althing – the world's first parliament. This marked the first evidence of some kind of democracy in many parts of Europe. The parliament of Iceland is still known as the Althing.

The early Althing was held outdoors in a place now known as Thingvellir ('Thing Fields') in Iceland.

Feuds and fines

One of the biggest problems in Scandinavia in Viking times was the 'blood feud'. This was when the victim of a crime or their family reacted by attacking the person who had done the deed. Blood feuds could result in years of violence.

To prevent blood feuds, the Vikings introduced fines as a punishment for crimes such as stealing. The local Thing would decide on suitable compensation for the victim. When the Vikings settled in England and France, they took this idea with them and it soon spread to other parts of Europe. Fines are still a common form of punishment for minor crimes today.

WOW!

Although Viking women were not allowed to vote at a Thing, they enjoyed more freedom than most women at the time. When their menfolk were off exploring or raiding, women ran the farms. They were allowed to own land and could divorce their husbands.

The Jónsbók is the book of Icelandic law, first compiled in 1281.

LANGUAGE

Many words in the modern English language can be traced back to the Vikings. Their influence can also still be seen in a lot of place names, especially in areas where many Vikings settled.

GENIUS ★ LEGACY OF WORDS

WOW!

Viking and Anglo-Saxon poets used kennings, a word that comes from the Old Norse *kenna* ('to know'). Kennings describe things as if they were something else. For example, the kennings 'whale road,' 'bed of fish' and 'land of the ocean noise' all describe the sea.

Merging cultures

The people who lived in England when the Vikings first arrived spoke a language we now call Old English. At first there was not much interaction between the two cultures, but later the Vikings began to mingle more with the Anglo-Saxons. As the two groups traded, settled and intermarried, the Norse and English languages began to mix.

The Vikings learned words from other languages so that they could communicate with visitors to trading posts, such as the one pictured here.

Viking words

Words that come from the Old Norse include many that begin with 'sk', including 'ski', 'sky', 'skin' and 'skill'. Several words that start with the letters 'thr' are also of Viking origin, such as 'thrust', 'thrall', 'thrift'.

Place names

As they settled in England, the Vikings named their own villages and communities — usually after local land features or the person who ruled an area. There were several words for 'village' or 'farm' in Old Norse, including *by* and *thorpe*. These have survived in place names such as Grimsby and Scunthorpe.

TEST OF TIME

The Vikings named the days of the week after their gods. This influence is still evident in some of the English names.

Sunday: named after Sunni (or Sol), the Norse personification of the Sun.

Monday: named after Mani, the Norse personification of the Moon.

Tuesday: named after the Norse god Tyr, who was associated with law and heroism.

Wednesday: named after the chief Norse god Woden, or Odin.

Thursday: named after Thor, the Norse god of thunder, strength and protection.

Friday: named after Odin's wife, the goddess Freya.

Saturday: the Vikings kept the Roman name for this day!

The Norse god Odin was associated with victory, death and wisdom.

SKIING

Although no one knows for sure when or where people first began to ski, the western tradition of skiing for both enjoyment and transport has been traced back to early Scandinavian people.

Skis helped the Vikings to get around more easily in their snowy homeland.

An ancient form of transport

Skiing was one of the earliest forms of transport, and people in Scandinavia have probably skied for around 5,000 years. There are rock carvings in Norway showing people on sledges and wearing skis. However, the Vikings were the first to use modern-style skis and poles.

TEST OF TIME

The word 'ski' comes from the old Norse word 'skid', which means 'stick of wood'.

Skiing deities

The Vikings even worshipped gods of skiing who were depicted on skis or snowshoes. For example, Skadi was the goddess of hunting with a bow and of skiing. She is often shown on skis. Ullr was the god of hunting, the shield and snow shoes!

This manuscript illustration shows the Norse god Ullr on his skis.

The Reinheimen ski

A 1,300-year-old ski made of birch wood was recently discovered in Reinheimen, Norway. It told experts much more about the Vikings' practice of skiing than they had ever known before. The Reinheimen ski was the first to be found with the binding intact. From this, we know that the Vikings made the binding of wicker and leather. We also know roughly how big the Vikings made their skis.

(((BRAIN WAVE)))

Overland travel in Scandinavia was easier in winter than in summer. Then, the Vikings could cross frozen lakes and rivers. Sledges have been found in Viking burial sites, which experts believe were used to pull cargo around in winter.

PERSONAL GROOMING

The Vikings have a reputation as bloodthirsty barbarians, so you wouldn't think they were the type of people who would care much about how they looked. But items found in Viking graves suggest that the Vikings did take personal grooming and hygiene seriously!

Many combs found in Viking graves are beautifully decorated, which suggests that they were valued belongings.

Deer-antler combs

Primitive combs have been found in other, earlier, cultures, but the Vikings are believed to have been the first to use the type of comb familiar to us today. They were usually made from deer antlers. The Vikings are thought to have worn them on a belt, alongside a sword or knife, and took them when they sailed off on voyages of exploration or plunder.

WOW!

Among the items found in Viking burial sites are tiny spoons thought to be used for scooping wax out of the ears.

Blond is best

The Vikings considered fair hair to be more attractive than dark. To lighten their hair, they washed it in a type of soap made with lye, which acted like bleach. Men also used this special soap on their beards. This treatment may have had the added benefit of getting rid of head lice!

TEST OF TIME

The Vikings wore spectacles, making glass lenses out of crushed rock dust. These glasses couldn't have been used to improve eyesight though, so it seems more likely that the Vikings wore them as a fashion statement!

The blacksmith's grave

In 2014, the grave of a Viking blacksmith was discovered in Sogndalsdalen, Norway. It contained about 60 different items and revealed a lot about the role and status of blacksmiths in Viking society. As well as his weapons and the tools of his trade, the blacksmith was buried with many personal items. These included a razor, tweezers, scissors for trimming his beard and a comb made from bone.

Items like these such as buckles and jewellery found at burial sites give us a glimpse into the personal habits of the Vikings.

VIKING SAGAS

A saga is a tale that tells of the heroic deeds of Viking families. The Viking sagas cannot be taken as a completely reliable source of information, but they have given us a lot of information about Viking life and culture.

What are the sagas?

The Icelandic sagas were written between the twelfth and the fourteenth centuries, but they record events that took place between around CE 900 and 1000. This was the time when the Vikings were turning away from their pagan gods and towards Christianity.

TEST OF TIME

It has been suggested that the Icelandic sagas – with their dramatic storylines and larger-than-life characters – are an early form of soap opera!

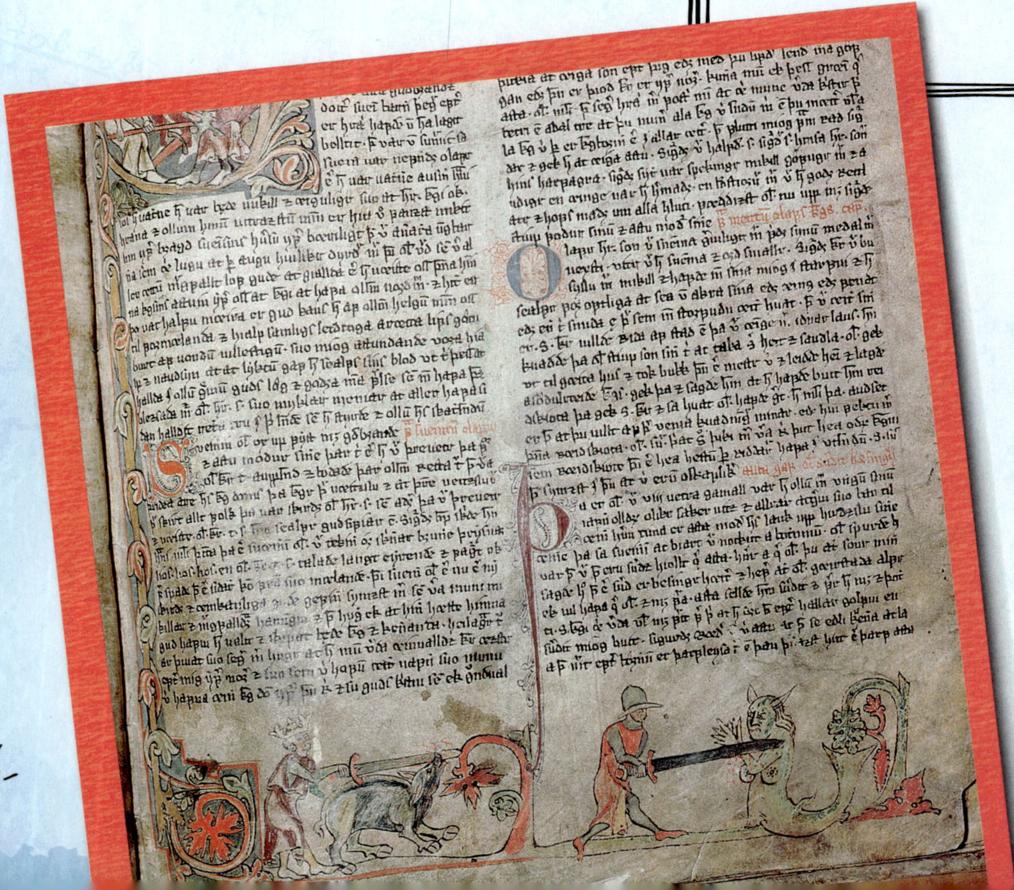

This is a page from the saga called the Flateyjarbok, which includes tales about Icelandic saints and heroes.

An epic tale

The Saga of Erik the Red, written sometime before 1265, is mainly about the Vikings' discovery of North America. It describes how Erik was banished from Iceland, then tells of how his son Leif Eriksson discovered Vinland (see page 13). Despite its title, the main characters are Thorfinn Karlsefni and his wife Gudrid, who carried on Leif's exploration.

One family's story

Egil's Saga, written around 1240, is a history of Egil Skallagrimsson, who was a farmer and a poet. The saga begins with Egil's grandfather, Ulf, and describes how he and his two sons left Norway for Iceland. The rest of the saga spans 150 years, telling the family's story down to Egil's own children.

WOW!

Most sources that were written during the Viking era, including the *Anglo-Saxon Chronicle*, depict the Norsemen as cruel and bloodthirsty raiders. That's because they were written by the victims of Viking raids. The icelandic sagas present a different side to the Vikings, giving us a more balanced view.

This sculpture of Bardur Snaesfellas is in Iceland. Bardur, half human, half giant, is the hero of the Icelandic saga that bears his name.

GLOSSARY

binding — the part of a ski attached to the flat base that covers the foot

colonise — to settle in and take political control of another country

commodity — something that can be bought and sold

compensation — money or goods awarded to someone to pay them back for loss or injury

conquer — to take control of a foreign land, usually by force

exile — when someone is sent away from their home or country as punishment for a crime

hull — the main part of a ship, including the sides, bottom and deck

latitude — a measure of an object's position north or south of the Equator

mast — a tall upright post on a boat that the sail is attached to

native — describing something or someone that comes from a particular place

pagan — someone who does not follow one of the world's main religions; often from an ancient culture that worshipped lots of different gods

plundering — stealing goods by force, often in time of war

primitive — an early version of something

rivet — a metal bolt or pin used for holding wood or metal together

rudder — the steering device on a boat

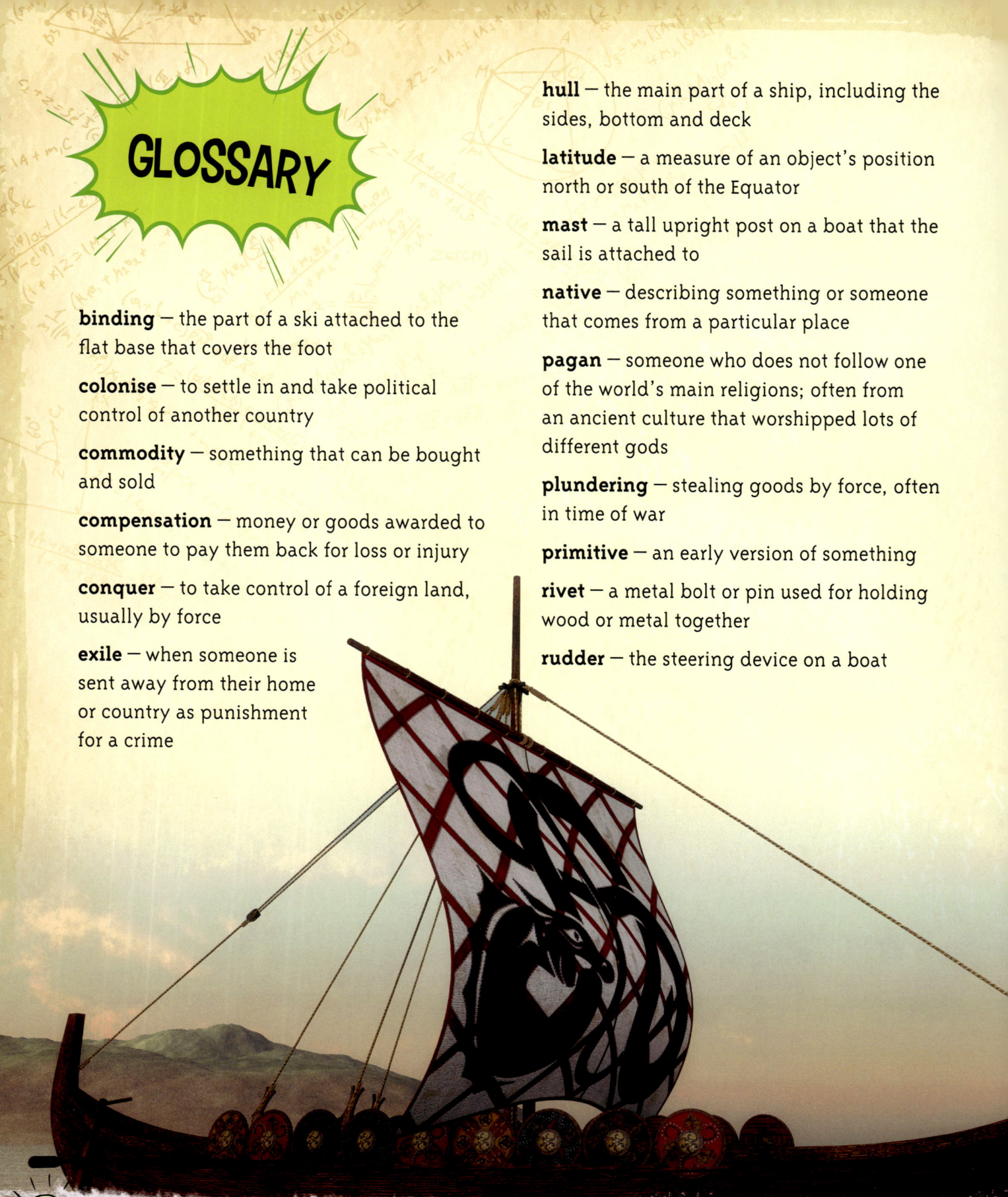

TIMELINE

CE 793	First raid on England, at Lindisfarne.
CE 865	A large Viking army invades England.
CE 867	The Vikings make Jorvik (York) their capital.
CE 886	Alfred, king of Wessex, makes a deal with the Vikings that they can live in an area that becomes known as the Danelaw.
CE 927	Athelstan captures the Danelaw and becomes the first king of all England.
CE 954	Eric Bloodaxe, the last Viking king in England, is driven out of Jorvik by King Eadred of Wessex.
1013	Viking Swein Forkbeard drives out Ethelred the Unready and becomes king of England.
1016	Danish king Canute becomes ruler of England.
1042	Anglo-Saxons choose an English king after the death of Canute's sons.
1066	The Norman invasion drives back the last serious Viking threat when Harald Hardraada is killed.

INDEX

Alfred, King of Wessex 5, 31
Althing, the 20
Anglo-Saxons 5, 14, 22, 31

battle-axes 16–17
blood feuds 21

combs 26, 27
compasses 10–11, 12

Danelaw 5, 20, 31

Eriksson, Leif 13, 29
Erik the Red 13, 29
exploration 8, 9, 10, 12–13, 26

fines 21
fire 13

gods 23, 25, 28
Greenland 13

helmets 4, 16

Iceland 12, 13, 20, 21, 28, 29

kennings 22

language 4, 20, 22–23, 24
laws 20–21
longships 6–7, 8, 9, 12, 18

Oseberg Ship 9

raids 5, 8, 9, 31

sagas 12, 28–29
Scandinavia 4, 8, 9, 11, 13, 20, 21, 24, 25
shields 16, 17, 18–19
skiing 24–25
slaves 15
spectacles 27
Svavarsson, Gardar 12

Things 20, 21
trade 5, 9, 10, 14–15, 22

Vinland 13

weapons 16, 17

Websites

www.bbc.co.uk/schools/primaryhistory/vikings/who_were_the_vikings/

www.dkfindout.com/uk/history/vikings/

www.primaryhomeworkhelp.co.uk/vikings.html

Books

Everyday Life, Art and Culture (Discover the Vikings) by John C. Miles (Franklin Watts, 2018)

Vikings (Found!) by Moira Butterfield (Franklin Watts, 2017)

Warriors, Exploration and Trade (Discover the Vikings) by John C. Miles (Franklin Watts, 2018)

The Vikings (Britain in the Past) by Moira Butterfield (Franklin Watts, 2017)

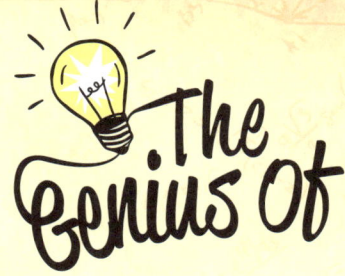

Titles in the series

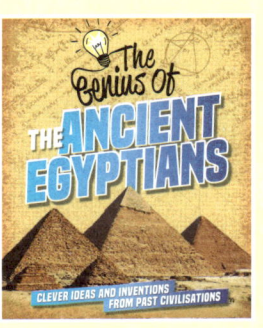

- Who were the Egyptians?
- Pyramids • Temples
- Writing • Papyrus
- Farming methods
- Irrigation • Calendars
- Clocks • Mummification
- Medicine • Toothpaste
- Cosmetics

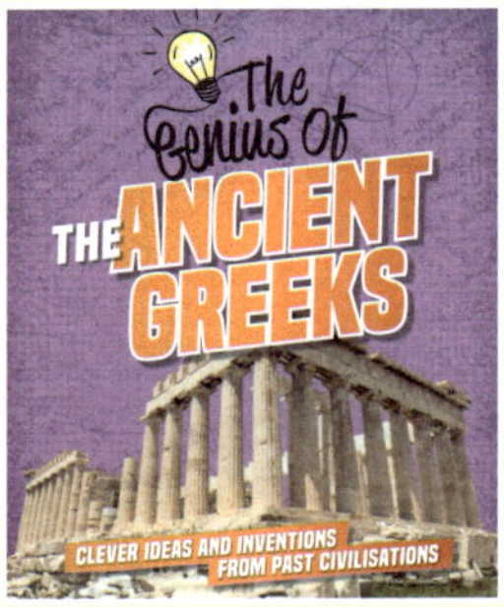

HB 9781445161198
PB 9781445161204

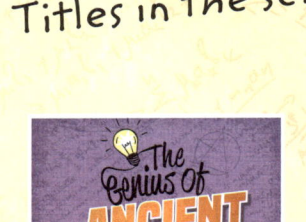

- The Greeks • The Empire
- Democracy • Sports
- Medicine • Philosophy
- Warfare • Buildings
- Theatre • Science • Maths
- Art • Astronomy

HB 9781445161211
PB 9781445161228

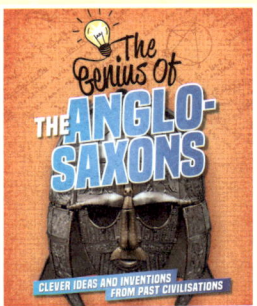

- The Anglo-Saxons
- Kingdoms and rulers
- Society • Towns • Laws
- Old English • Trade
- Art • Food • Defence
- Weapons and armour
- Entertainment • Clothes

HB 9781445161174
PB 9781445161181

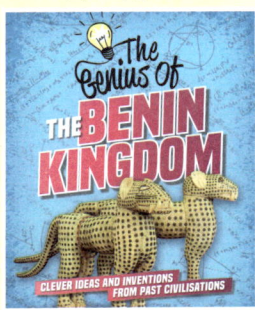

- What was the Benin Kingdom? • Powerful leaders • The city-state
- Professional soldiers
- Farming • Trade • Town planning • Craft guilds
- Art • Metalwork
- Working with wood
- Textiles • Botany

HB 9781445161259
PB 9781445161266

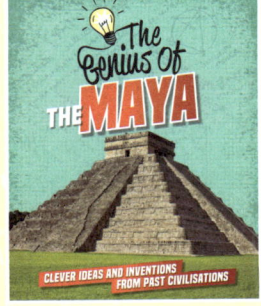

- The Maya • Government and kings • Trade • Warfare
- Cities • Buildings
- Writing • Food
- The Mayan calendar
- Astronomy • Sports
- Art • Clothes

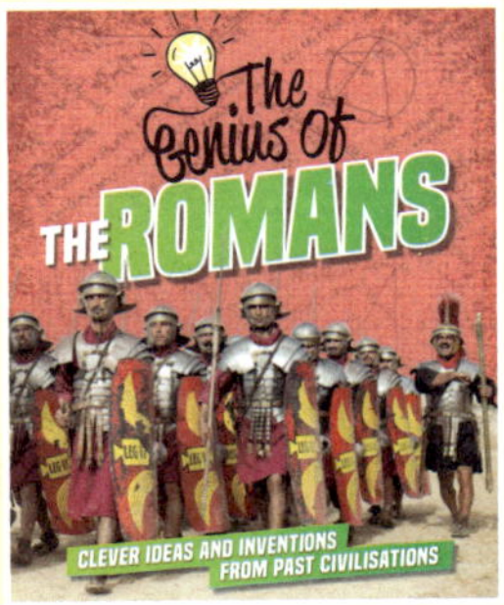

HB 9781445161235
PB 9781445161242

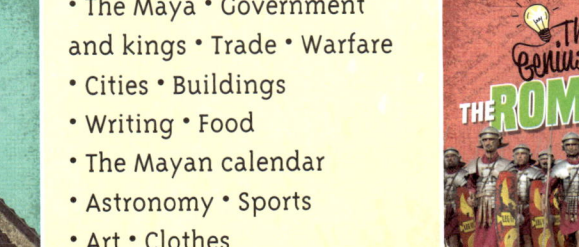

- The Romans • The army
- Trade • Concrete • Roads
- Water • Calendars • Food
- The Latin language
- Government • Laws
- City services • Show time!

HB 9781445161129
PB 9781445161136

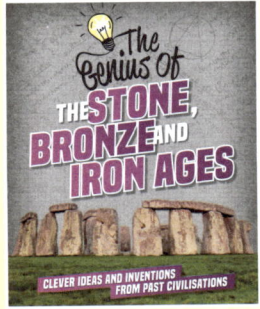

- The Stone, Bronze and Iron Ages • Stone
- Bronze • Iron • Farming
- Construction
- Settlements • Society
- Trade • Clothing • Art
- The wheel • Writing

HB 9781445160467
PB 9781445160474

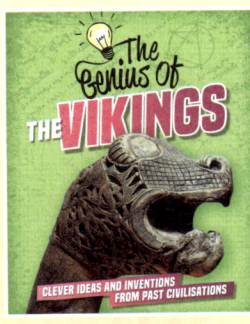

- The Vikings • The Viking longship • Sails and keels
- Compasses • Exploration
- Trade • Battle-axes
- Shields • Law and democracy • Language
- Skiing • Personal grooming • Viking sagas

HB 9781445161167
PB 9781445161143